# Change:
## Coping with Tomorrow Today

Written by Patricia Wilson
Edited by National Press Publications

NATIONAL PRESS PUBLICATIONS
A Division of Rockhurst College Continuing Education Center, Inc.
6901 West 63rd Street • P.O. Box 2949 •
Shawnee Mission, Kansas 66201-1349
1-800-258-7248 • 1-913-432-7757

National Seminars endorses nonsexist language.
However, in an effort to make this handbook clear,
consistent and easy to read, we've used the generic
"he" throughout when referring to both males and
females. The copy is not intended to be sexist.

### *Change: Coping with Tomorrow Today*

ISBN 1-55852-109-7

# Change:
# Coping with Tomorrow Today
How to Handle the Challenge of Change

## Table of Contents

# Introduction

---

*"Change is the process by which the future invades our lives..."*
**— Alvin Toffler**

Remember when...

- life was made up of simple choices?

    — Ford or Chevy?

    — chocolate ice cream or vanilla?

    — working 9 to 5 or not at all?

- loyalty meant always having a job?

- the ladder of success was climbed one rung at a time?

- the boss held your career in HIS hands?

- education was something you got before you were 21?

- you weren't supposed to challenge "the rules"?

- a career was meant to last a lifetime?

It's all changed, hasn't it?  The business world we work in today bears little resemblance to the business world of just a few years ago — a world that many of us entered with high hopes and shining ambition. CHANGE has invaded that world and turned it upside down. Now...

- there are multitudes of choices for everything, from the flavor of your ice cream to the hours you wish to work.

- neither companies nor employees expect loyalty to guarantee a job.

- the ladder of success has been replaced by a leapfrog maze with no clear direction.

- the boss may be male or female, and YOU hold your career in your own hands.

- education is an ongoing process.

- the rules are there to be challenged.

- you may change careers several times in your lifetime.

John Naisbitt, in his book *Megatrends,* summed it up beautifully. "Although the time between eras is uncertain, it is a great and yeasty time, filled with opportunity. If we can learn to make uncertainty our friend, we can achieve more than in stable eras.

"In stable eras, everything has a name and everything knows its place, and we can leverage very little. But [now] we have extraordinary leverage and influence — individually, professionally, and institutionally — if we can only get a clear sense, a clear conception, a clear vision, of the road ahead!"

This book will help you get that "clear sense, clear conception, and clear vision of the road ahead."

# 1

## LIFE JUST KEEPS ON CHANGING

### Fifty Years of Change

Most of us wish that change would just go away!  As soon as we begin to feel comfortable and at ease with our world, along comes change, and it seems we've got to start all over again. But change is not going to go away. In fact, when we consider the last 50 years, change has been coming at an astonishing rate. For instance, since 1942, we've invented:

- artificial hearts, organ transplants and The Pill

- radar, television and FM radio

- nuclear energy, laser beams, credit cards and ballpoint pens

- frozen food, air conditioners and drip-dry clothes

- pantyhose to replace stockings, clothes dryers to replace clotheslines and electric blankets to replace feather beds

Because of these things and countless more, our lives have changed dramatically. In many instances, the typical family of the '50s has been replaced by single-parent homes and commuter marriages. Holidays no longer are spent in a leisurely drive across the country, but often in a time-shared condo. We rely on daycare centers, nursing homes and group support sessions to help us deal with our family and personal needs.

Sometimes, the only thing we can count on is change!

The changes of the last 50 years all have been piecemeal, usually unrelated to each other. But there is another kind of change taking place in our society today that affects every aspect of our lives: *We are undergoing a shift in our belief about what constitutes power.*

## Muscle

In the beginning, our civilization believed that power came from MUSCLE. The leader with the biggest army, the most weapons and the greatest desire to conquer emerged as the most powerful. Attila the Hun, Charlemagne, Alexander the Great, Julius Caesar — their names have gone down in history as they seized the power that their muscle afforded them.

## Money

Later, the world underwent a power shift. MONEY became the basis of power. The wealthiest, the richest, the most financially secure were on top. First the great land barons, then the factory owners and the industrialists, and then the financiers ruled with their wealth. Their names were watchwords for power: Donald Trump, Robert Campeau and the Reichmann brothers.

But their glory is fading, too, as these mighty financiers have fallen prey to our changing economy. The properties that they owned and used as collateral to finance other ventures have lost their value as real estate prices continue to fall. This, in turn, affects the stock market, and junk bonds issued by the financiers become worthless. The millionaires are millionaires only on paper.

## Information

The new basis for power is INFORMATION. Muscle and money have given way to the information age. Those who continuously adapt, use new ideas, learn new technologies, systems and applications, as well as those who know how to access the information and use it are the owners of future power. To use the resources of the information age, to supply innovative, appropriate and timely service to customers' problems are the true marks of success.

## Living 100 Years in 10

Everyone agrees that the world is rapidly changing.
According to futurist Faith Popcorn, change will
continue to accelerate. She believes that we will
change as much in the next 10 years as we have in the
last 50, and as much again in the five years following
that. Consider the ramifications:

1940 — 1990 = 50 YEARS OF CHANGE

1990 — 2000 = 50 YEARS OF CHANGE

2000 — 2005 = 50 YEARS OF CHANGE

## The Bottom Line?

IF YOU PLAN TO LIVE FOR ANOTHER 15 YEARS,
YOU ACTUALLY WILL LIVE THROUGH 100 YEARS
OF CHANGE!

Given these prospects, we might as well learn how to
use the changes around us to enhance our lives and
increase our successes.

## Reacting to the "Change Vehicle"

Change is like a car coming down the street toward you. It has no driver that you can see, but it is moving surely and steadily in your direction. You have three options:

1. **Reactive:**  Jump out of the way. The car will pass you by. You may realize too late that it was going in the direction you hoped to follow.

2. **Nonactive:**  Stand still. The car will run over you and leave you behind, probably in worse condition than before the encounter.

3. **Proactive:**  Start to move along with the car. Match speed, then jump into the driver's seat so that you can steer the car where you want to go.

How we handle change in our lives depends entirely upon our reaction to the change vehicle. We can be proactive, reactive or nonactive. But we cannot ignore the fact that change vehicles will keep appearing in our lives.

## The Circle of Change

Change is inevitable. Nothing can exist without change. Without change, a seed never would become a plant, a flower never would bloom, and seeds never would be created to form the next plant. Without change, life simply would cease.

There are three constant or steadfast factors of change:

1.  Change is a reality in any living organism.

2.  Being a problem-solver means more change.

3.  The continuous circle of change cannot be ignored.

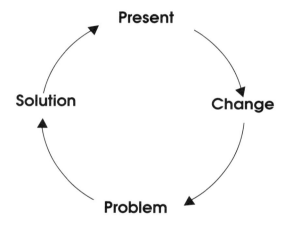

In our lives, change usually brings a new series of challenges or problems, depending upon our point of view. Let's examine something as commonplace as weight gain.

*   If we put on a few pounds (change), then we are faced with a challenge. Nothing fits (problem). Something must be done (solution).

- We meet the change challenge by going on a diet (present reality).

- The diet raises a whole new series of challenges, such as cutting back on snacks, which we must deal with and solve. This, in turn, creates another present reality.

As you can see, the change cycle is never-ending.

Here's another example.

- Your company uses a manual system of invoicing (present reality).

- The invoices are not getting out on time, so data processing is introduced (change).

- The employees do not know how to use the new technology (challenge/problem).

- Retraining is scheduled (solution).

- The invoices are electronically handled (present reality).

- Some invoices do not meet the criteria of the new system (change).

- A new system must be designed (problem).

...and so the circle goes on. How you deal with the change circle will determine how successfully you manage change. Remember, the one thing that you cannot do is ignore the circle of change!

This handbook will help you deal with change proactively. You will learn how to use change as a vehicle to take you to your chosen destination. More importantly, you will learn how to see change as an opportunity for your professional and personal success.

# 2

## CHANGE CAN BE POSITIVE

### What Is That Light at the End of the Tunnel?

Someone once paraphrased the well-known poem "If" by Rudyard Kipling as follows, "If you can keep your head when all others about you are losing theirs, then you obviously don't know the gravity of the situation." Or to put it another way, "If you see a light at the end of the tunnel, it's probably the train coming toward you!"

These attitudes are the ones that prevent us from dealing with change comfortably. In our heart of hearts, we are convinced that those who extol the virtues of change simply don't understand the gravity of the situation and those who eagerly point to the light at the end of the tunnel haven't realized that it is the train coming toward them!

We believe that the Pollyannas of the world ignore the
negative aspects of change because they don't want to
take off their rose-colored glasses long enough to get
a realistic look at what is coming.

## Positive Focus

What we need is a way to focus on the opportunities
that change may bring, rather than on the negative
aspects of change that tend to color our perceptions.

By honestly evaluating change and how it will affect
us, both personally and professionally, we can begin
to deal with it from a rational rather than an emotional
viewpoint.

When we put the actual change down on paper, we
can begin to see its true outline. Dealing with change
in black and white, rather than as a nebulous feeling,
forces us to see the change as it really is. We still may
not like what we see, but the change becomes a
concrete structure that we can begin to address.

Two simple steps will help us put the change into
perspective and give us a structure for dealing with it.
These two steps describe the change and determine its
source.

## Step One: Describe the Change

First, develop a complete description of the change.

- What triggered it? What happened or is happening that caused this change to be considered?

- What is the exact nature of the change that is being proposed or implemented?

- How does this change affect your responsibilities? What specific issues will the change directly affect?

- Who is responsible for implementing the change?

- What monitoring will be carried out to assure implementation of the change?

## Step Two: Recognize the Imposition

Imposition is a great word that simply means, "who is pushing for the change"? How we deal with change depends a great deal on who has decided that the change must occur.

There are four possibilities:

1. The boss (or management)

2. The system

3. The customer

4. Self

## Boss- or Management-Imposed Change

Let's start with a boss-imposed change. Often, this type of change occurs when a new boss appears on the scene or when two companies merge into one. It's not just a matter of a new broom sweeping clean. It's more a matter of fresh eyes viewing the old scene and seeing clearly where changes will benefit the organization. Obviously, for the employee, a boss-imposed change creates a lot of questions.

- Can I do this?

  There is often a real fear that we won't be able to do what is being asked of us. Worse, we suspect that we will be judged by how we handle the change and that our jobs may be on the line.

- Am I the one to do this?

  Sometimes new management teams are not aware of each individual employee's job responsibilities, and in their eagerness to move along change, therefore, they may wrongly assign change tasks.

- Does my job need to be redefined?

  If the boss or management does not want to reassign a change task, it may be necessary to redefine the job description to accommodate the change.

- Is retraining/education available to help me deal with the change?

  Rather than risk failure because of lack of knowledge, it is to your advantage to ask for or seek out retraining opportunities to deal with a boss-imposed change.

- Do I have any negotiation leverage in this change?

  Can you use your knowledge, expertise, interpersonal skills, leadership abilities, group dynamics or willingness to change as negotiation points in bringing about the change that the boss or management desires? Can these points position you so you will receive a bonus from the change: promotion, salary increase, special training or overtime privileges?

## Example

The new boss in your department has decided that all customer service calls no longer will go through a central operator, but will be routed directly to the next available customer service representative. The reason for the change is that too many calls are put on hold while the operator tries to deal with the current call and route it to a service expert. Ask yourself these questions about the proposed change.

- Can I do this?

  Yes. I can take the calls as they come. However, I'm uncomfortable with the idea of handling calls that are not from my regular customer service base.

- Am I the one to do this?

  No, not always. I have the knowledge and background for certain areas of customer service, but my colleagues always have handled other customer service areas.

- Does my job need to be redefined?

  No. My job is customer service, and I still will be doing that.

- Is retraining/education available to help me deal with the change?

  Not formally. However, I will suggest that we begin some kind of information exchange among customer service representatives so that all of us can handle customers who have needs in areas outside our expertise. I would like to be retrained in the other areas as well. This would make me much more valuable to the company and much more responsive to the customer.

- Do I have any negotiation leverage in this change?

  I'm pretty good at organizing. I think I can convince my boss that I would be able to organize the information exchange program with my colleagues. That also might give me some leverage into the training division of this company. Maybe I can move from customer service into a more specialized area.

## System-Imposed Change

A system-imposed change is the most common way of encountering change. The system just doesn't work anymore. Remember the old-style system of bookkeeping with hand-written entries in a number of journals, manual accounts payable/receivable systems and hand-written checks? It's just not adequate for today's larger organization with hundreds of customers and thousands of accounts. We've moved from the original journal entry system to computerized financial systems that can handle any number of accounts. The system CHANGED because of a system-imposed need. This type of change also creates a lot of questions.

- Is this within my responsibility?

  This is probably the hardest question to deal with in a system-imposed change. Often, we see changes that could improve the system, but unless we have the responsibility and/or authority for that part of the system, we cannot directly affect the change. Instead, we must convince those who do have the responsibility and/or authority to make the change.

• Is it worth doing?

Change just for the sake of change is not good. There are people who just enjoy making changes, but unless those changes will have a measurable, positive influence on the system, they are not worth doing.

• Can this be referred somewhere else?

Who is ultimately responsible for the area in which the change needs to take place? That person or department probably is already aware of the problem, but has no solution yet. Often, outsiders can see ways to improve a system because they are not actively involved in thinking "that's the way we've always done it." Offering a solution, rather than complaining about a problem, is a positive way to deal with a failing system.

• Do I have time? Do others?

The one factor that often is overlooked when implementing change is the time needed to learn. All change takes time. Some changes are better left until the time is right.

## Example

You see bottlenecks in the shipping system used by your company. As a result, your customers do not receive their orders as promised. This has added to your customer service complaints. However, you think that you have a solution to the bottleneck.

- Is this within my responsibility?

  No. Not at all. I am in customer service. However, I do have a responsibility to customers, and they are the ones who are affected by shipping delays.

- Is it worth doing?

  Absolutely. It will make a great difference in our sales if we deliver as promised, and it will eliminate a lot of headaches in the other departments.

- Can this be referred somewhere else?

  People in the shipping department have heard our complaints time and time again. They say there is no way to change the system. I need to put my ideas down on paper, show exactly how the change will work and give some suggestions for putting it into effect.

- Do I have time? Do others?

    I'm just as busy as everyone else. But I know
    I'm wasting a lot of time on these shipping
    delays. I also know that it will take time to
    implement a new system. So I need to wait for
    the right time to bring this idea to the shipping
    department. I won't expect workers there to
    overhaul the shipping system in the middle of
    the busiest shipping period of the year. I can
    wait until the slow period to suggest
    implementing the change. Change does not
    respond well to time pressures, and if I push it
    now, we probably will run into even more
    problems.

### Customer-Imposed Change

Some change is imposed by the customer. When a
company realizes that its customers are not happy and
that they will be lost if something is not done, the
company will make a change. To make a change that
will satisfy both the customer and the company, a
number of questions should be raised.

- Can I do what the customer wants?

    "The customer is always right" — the credo for
    many organizations — does not necessarily
    mean that the customer's desire for change is
    also realistic. A customer may want 24-hour
    repair service, but that may be impossible with
    the existing number of repair personnel.

- What is the bottom-line impact?

  Sometimes what the customer wants is possible only by changing the bottom line. To use the previous example, a 24-hour repair service may be posssible if six extra people are hired. But, can the organization handle the expense of six extra people and still offer the same pricing structure to the customer?

- Will I keep my customer?

  If the bottom-line impact means a higher cost to the customer, even a customer-imposed change does not necessarily mean that you will keep that customer. It's a Catch-22 situation for business. Only after calculating the dollars and cents needed to make the change and weighing that amount against the customer's needs and expectations can a manager decide to impose this type of change.

## Self-Imposed Change

We do impose change on ourselves — even changes that we do not like. Anyone who ever has gone on a diet knows this! In business, some of us have made the transition from manual typewriters to word processors; some of us have voluntarily gone back to school and retrained; some of us have moved out of comfortable careers into new fields of endeavor. Change is often self-imposed. The negative impact of these changes can be lessened if we prepare ourselves by anticipating any difficulties.

- How will this affect the work I'm doing?

  Before we can begin to implement any change, we must assess the damage that will be done to our current work. In most cases, the quality of our work will suffer initially because of experimenting, making mistakes and starting over. This means that we must allow more time for the work affected by the change. We also must prepare ourselves and others for possible problem areas during the initial implementation of the change.

- Can I control this?

  If your work will be affected by the change, it is essential that you have some degree of control over it. You need to have the flexibility to work with the change: adapting, discarding and reinventing as you go along. If you set yourself up for a rigid change — one that must be done in a certain way, in a certain time-frame, in a certain order — you are, in effect, boxing yourself in by this change. The change controls you and your actions.

- Can parts of the change be delegated?

  In a perfect world, there always would be people to whom we could delegate. In actuality, there are seldom any opportunities for us to delegate. We often end up with the whole burden of self-imposed change on our shoulders. However, delegation often can take the form of persuasion. If we can convince others of the need for change, we often can persuade them to take responsibility for some aspects of it.

• What are the opportunities? How do I create winners?

The principle of WIIFM (what's in it for me) applies here. If the change is self-imposed, then you already know what's in it for you. But, to convince others to participate actively in the change, you first must convince them that there is something in it for them, too. Look at the change condition from the perspective of others. What opportunities exist for them?

— How can they gain skills, energy, time, power or position?

— What can they use to make their jobs easier?

— What aspect of the change can they own?

## Example

Suppose you have made the decision to upgrade your skills. The course that you need is only available during regular working hours. Because it is directly related to your job responsibilities, the company has agreed to pay for the course and allow you time off but only if it will not affect your normal work.

- How will this affect the work you're doing?

  Although the course is only one afternoon a week, it's the afternoon when you've always updated the weekly sales figures. The sales department uses these figures to monitor sales activity and to set goals, incentives and deadlines. You're going to have to find a way to get the weekly updates done, finish all the rest of your work and do your course assignments.

- Can you control this?

  You're feeling a little boxed in because you can't change the course time, you must do the assignments, and you can't do the weekly updates any earlier. The only thing you can control is your time management. You know that you can have the weekly update prepared so that the addition of the final figures can be done in about 20 minutes. You'll plan to do that in the morning, but you'll need to find someone who will put in those final figures and run a print-out.

- Can parts be delegated?

  No one can be delegated to do your work. You don't have the authority. You need to convince someone that it would be to his or her advantage to help you with the weekly updates.

- What are the opportunities? How do you create winners?

  First of all, who possibly could benefit from inputting the weekly update figures? On first thought, no one. But on second thought, two of your colleagues might like an opportunity to learn weekly updating since they aspire to sales positions. Come to think of it, some of the newer sales people might appreciate the chance to see the figures ahead of anyone else. They aren't a secret, but seeing the actual figures might give them an edge.

## The Light at the End of the Tunnel

The light at the end of the change tunnel is not the train coming toward you. It is the daylight of mental, emotional and physical preparation for change.

You create daylight at the end of the change tunnel by focusing on the opportunities that the change can bring you and by preparing yourself for the change.

# 3

## CHANGE CONDITIONS YOU JUST CAN'T IGNORE

Although everything from gaining weight to introducing a new way of doing our jobs can trigger the circle of change in our lives, five key conditions in today's world always demand our attention. They affect us in almost every aspect of our professional lives. They are:

- TECHNOLOGY

- PROSPERITY POCKETS

- COMPETITION

- HUMAN CAPITAL

- INDIVIDUAL RESPONSIBILITY

## Technology — Tools of the Information Age

Modern technology has enabled us to gather and disseminate information at a greater pace. One issue of the *New York Times* now contains more information than a Renaissance man would have read in his entire lifetime!

Dr. Robert Hilliard presses the point further: "At the rate at which knowledge is growing, by the time the child born today graduates from college, the amount of knowledge in the world will be four times as great. By the time the same child is 50 years old, it will be 32 times as great and 97 percent of everything known in the world will have been learned since the time the child was born."

What does this mean to us? Quite simply, we are suffering from information overload. Daily, we access and process information from a variety of different technologies.

- MEDIA: newspapers, magazines, radio and television

- DATA COMMUNICATIONS: electronic mail, paging systems, telex, point-of-sale debit systems, electronic banking, facsimile machines and bar-code scanners

- OFFICE COMPUTERS: word-processing, desktop publishing, graphics, project management, data base management software, spreadsheet and financial software and "what-if" scenarios

- PRINTED COMMUNICATIONS: plotters, slides, copiers and high-speed printers

- VOICE COMMUNICATIONS: telephones, cellular phones, voice mail systems, telemarketing and computer bulletin boards

The information comes at us from every direction! Once we receive the information, we must sort and prioritize.

What can we use?

What do we need today?

What should we save in case we need it tomorrow?

Then, we must put the saved information to use by learning, practicing, trying and experimenting. The new information is assimilated gradually into our daily behavior. And all the while, new information continues to pour in. The same accessing, processing and assimilation occurs over and over again.

Somewhere between the speed and volume of the information presented to us and its short shelf life, we must deal with the knowledge that we haven't quite caught up. We realize that someone else is out in front, that we may have missed a vital piece of information they have and that we may be left behind.

## Prosperity Pockets: The Changing Economy

### Loss of Security

The volatile economy of the '80s and now of the '90s has given many of us a sense of uncertainty about our futures. As the cost of living goes up and the relative value of our wages goes down, we may feel that the security for which we have worked so long and hard slowly is seeping away.

### Loss of Upward Mobility

We watch with feelings of helplessness as fewer people have more power. The management jobs that were once part of our career plans are now jealously guarded by the incumbents. If an opening should occur, many others are equally qualified for the job. Upward mobility may seem unattainable.

### Increase in Demanding People

As job security lessens, the expectations of demanding people seem to increase. Now, more is expected of us: more time, more effort and more commitment to the organization. In return, we often feel that we receive less: less money, less satisfaction and less commitment from the organization. Career frustration proliferates.

## Competition: Inside and Outside

### Global Competition

Not only are we aware that there is increasing competition for the top jobs, but the shrinking world has created international competition for market share. Newly industrialized countries are able to compete favorably in world markets because they have combined low wages with new production and information technologies and sophisticated distribution methods. Just look at the labels in your clothes. They are made in Bangladesh, Mexico, Taiwan, India and Pakistan, as well as Canada, the United States and Great Britain. To counter this onslaught, the industrialized countries have been forced to adopt even newer technologies and to think globally.

### Demand for Value and Quality

You can buy roses from Bulgaria, cars from Japan and computers from Korea. Product loyalty no longer protects the manufacturer. Instead, the consumer looks for value and quality.

The rule used to be that if your dad always bought a Buick, so did you. Not today. You look for the car that combines value and quality. You want the biggest bang for your buck, and you buy accordingly. Now, interestingly, so does dad.

The concept of global thinking is not just for worldwide marketers of products and services. There's a need for global thinking within each of us personally, as well as at the company level. Global thinking, in a company sense, promotes greater communication among people within departments, divisions, branches and head offices. There is a realization that the one thing everyone has in common is the growth and prosperity of the company as a whole.

## Human Capital — People: The Evolution of Loyalty

Not so long ago, people expected to work for the same company for their entire working lives. At retirement, they received small pensions and gold watches for their efforts. Today, it is not uncommon to change employers, and even careers, several times during a working lifetime.

### Loyalty to Self

The sense of loyalty to one company has been replaced by loyalty to ourselves — to our personal goals, career plans and dreams. We choose to work for a company because it meets our individual needs. After time, if that company no longer meets those needs, we begin to look around for something else. If something else is not readily available, which is a reality in today's market, we simply bide our time until something else finally comes along. Some people spend an entire working lifetime waiting for something else! They live in a holding pattern, so their companies never receive 100 percent of their efforts.

## Company Loyalty

This lack of loyalty cuts both ways. If we no longer feel the sense of loyalty to the organization that our parents did, the organization no longer feels the same loyalty toward its employees. Companies now talk about and focus on the bottom line. If that means wage cutbacks, workforce reductions and layoffs, the company is prepared to make those changes.

## The Rise of the Specialist

Part of the reason for changing loyalties between employer and employee can be attributed to a fairly recent phenomenon: the rise of the specialist. The traditional corporate hierarchy is being invaded by hordes of experts — specialists in fields so narrow that often those at the top have difficulty understanding them. Increasingly, management has come to rely on the judgment of these experts — systems designers, operation researchers, engineering specialists and computer programmers.

These specialists, having assumed a vital role in the corporate world, now are able to sell their expertise to the highest bidders. Their loyalty to their own particular specialty supersedes any residual loyalty to their current organizations.

## Individual Responsibility

### Conflicting Management Styles

"If the trumpet sounds an uncertain note, who will follow?" asked Joshua. Now we hear uncertain and conflicting notes from people who lead the country, our organizations and our families. One group will tell us that the only way to economic security is to save as much as we can; another tells us that spending most of our disposable income is the route to economic recovery. Parents, in their uncertainty, follow the advice of experts by trying everything from strict, authoritarian childraising to allowing unlimited freedom. At times, it's difficult to know who or what to believe.

Never before has a society been faced with so many conflicting leadership styles:

Autocrats:      "Let's do it my way."

Democrats:      "Let's take a vote."

Technocrats:    "Let's give it to the computer to handle."

Theocrats:      "Let's ask the Higher Power, Inner Experience, Greater Good and/or Cosmic Consciousness."

Plutocrats:     "Let's let the richest and wealthiest handle it."

Bureaucrats:    "Let's follow the rule book."

Employees may leave a boss with one leadership style only to find that they must adjust to a new boss with a totally different style. Sometimes, if they work for multiple bosses, they will find themselves faced with conflicting messages.

**Conflicting Mission Statements**

Organizations are spending countless hours trying to define their mission statements. They ask:

Who are we?

Where are we going?

Why?

These questions often remain unanswered.

All this means that the trumpet call of management and leadership no longer is clarion clear. One moment we hear that service to the customer is most important. In the same breath we are told that our primary mission is to hold down expenses. Then we are offered a mission statement that expects us to become world leaders in our market. It's all very confusing.

**Lack of Decision-Making**

Conflicting expectations from upper management often are combined with wavering authority and uncertain decision-making. Because most organizations are now well-peppered with specialists, managers must rely increasingly on the judgment of these people. The specialists then assume a new decision-making role. At one time, they simply consulted with managers who reserved the final decision-making role for themselves. Now, however, as information and technology increase, these specialists stop merely advising and begin to make the decisions themselves.

Even if the managers have the final say, they often have to delay decision-making until they hear from the specialists. In fact, they are fearful of making a decision because they know that they do not have the working expertise to make it. They are caught by "paralysis of analysis" as they wait for more information before actually making a decision.

The trumpet note of today's business world never has been more uncertain!

## It's All in How You See It

Each day we all face these conditions of change in our lives. How we react to them determines whether we use the "change vehicle" to take us to our destinations, whether we will ignore it, or be run over by it.

Although change can be viewed pessimistically, **each of these conditions actually represents opportunities that are unparalleled in our history**. It is a matter of seeing these conditions in terms of how they affect our limits.

## Opportunity for Entrepreneurship

For some, economic uncertainties are a reason to withdraw, like a turtle surrounding itself by a protective shell. They hide under their shells, taking no risks, playing it safe, covering all the bases and staying well within their comfort zones.

Others see the convulsive economy as a glorious opportunity for entrepreneurship. The old rules no longer apply. "Nothing ventured; nothing gained," reminds them, as they boldly forge ahead, to use the changing economic conditions to create their own market niches. The increased competition for jobs excites them. They see the chance to shine and display their skills and talents in ways that will capture the imagination and attention of those who make promotion decisions. No longer contained by the traditional corporate movement of "one step up the hierarchical ladder at a time," they leapfrog over the shell-bound turtles!

The demand for doing more for less is just another challenge to these high flyers. They feel a great deal of personal satisfaction when they are able to use their resources in more efficient, economical ways.

Internal competition, external competition, loss of product loyalty, global competition — while all of these are red flags of danger to some, they act as beacons to others who plan to steer the change vehicle. They know that their limits are widening with new product markets and new people markets. They know if the service/quality/price mix is right, the market will buy.

## The Sky Is the Limit

The turtle feels especially ill at ease with the loss of security. What happened to the promise of a lifelong job? The turtles always have expected to enjoy what they considered their entitlements:

— a job

— security

— good wages

— a generous benefits package

— a pension at the end of their careers

When these entitlements are threatened by layoffs, reductions, downsizing, mergers and plant closings, what is a turtle to do?

Others will see these same conditions as an opportunity to step beyond the usual safe limits. They move into new fields, and if necessary, into new careers. They realize that the changing world of human capital means that their own specializations, acquired through retraining, will allow them to market their abilities to a wide variety of organizations. For them, the sky is the limit in this new marketplace.

## Vision for the Future

When they hear the turtles lamenting the lack of
leadership, lack of decision-making and lack of
management, the new entrepreneurs know that they
will supply the leadership and the vision for the
future.

Dealing with the change vehicle is all a matter of
perspective.

# 4

## FIVE STEPS TO
## CONQUER CHANGE

"No! No! No way! Not me! There's no way I'm going to
do that, accept that, give up that, CHANGE that!"
Sound familar? That's the typical first reaction when we
feel threatened by any of the conditions of change.

Whenever we are faced with any of the conditions of
change — technology, prosperity pockets, competition, human capital or individual responsibility — and
perceive them as threats in any way, we will deal with
them through a five-step process. These steps lead us
finally to accept and integrate the change into our
lives. Remember, it is only when we feel threatened by
change that we work through the five steps. If we are
not threatened, we take advantage of the change and
use it to suit our goals and purposes.

When office technology made the radical move from mechanical typewriters to computerized word-processing systems, people experienced the change condition in their daily lives. Either they welcomed the new technology or they feared it. Those who feared it went through the five steps: resistance, uncertainty, assimilation, transference and integration.

**Example:**

RESISTANCE:       "I can work just as well, just as fast and just as efficiently with my typewriter."

UNCERTAINTY:      "Well, maybe these new word processors would be good for form letters."

ASSIMILATION:     "I'm using the word processor, but don't take away my typewriter because I still use it when I'm in a hurry."

TRANSFERENCE:     "I wonder if I could do meeting notices on the word processor?"

INTEGRATION:      "I can't imagine trying to put out this volume of work using one of those manual typewriters!"

## Step One: Resistance

RESISTANCE comes from fear. When we feel that the change will affect our comfort zone in any way, we immediately begin to fear it. What we fear, we resist. Our resistance can take the form of loud vocal protests, specific activities aimed against the change (either open or subversive) or passive non-participation in the change.

Some people never move beyond resistance. They doggedly continue to resist the change long after it has become reality. We've all met the one person who still insists on using his old portable typewriter while everyone else in the office is plugged into a highly efficient word-processing system. These people have put themselves in an impossible position where they can't move on to the next step of accepting change.

Consider a change condition that feels threatening to you. Are you in the RESISTANCE stage of change? Ask yourself these questions:

- Do you let everyone around you know your negative feelings about the change?

- Do you have a million and one reasons why this change can't possibly work?

- Do you go out of your way to do things that will slow down or adversely affect the change?

## Step Two: Uncertainty

Eventually, everyone must see that the change has come to stay. Whether the resistance stage lasts three minutes or three years, the next step is inevitably UNCERTAINTY.

As we deal with change, this is probably the most uncomfortable step. The fear that we felt in the resistance stage provided an impetus that kept us going, but in the stage of uncertainty we experience stress.

Our comfort zone is being stretched by these nagging concerns.

- We wonder whether the change might work after all, and if it does work, will it work for us?

- We wonder if this change will leave us behind.

- We try to make sure the change will include us.

- We look for ways to use the change to our advantage.

- We have a lot of questions, but few answers.

Are you UNCERTAIN about a condition of change affecting you? Ask yourself these questions.

- Do you still feel hostility toward the change, but know that it is inevitable?

- Do you feel uncomfortable with the change, unsure, nervous, indecisive?

- Are you experiencing stress symptoms — physical, emotional or mental — that you attribute to the change?

## Step Three: Assimilation

Whether we like it or not, the change condition remains. Our state of uncertainty is replaced by a gradual ASSIMILATION of the new condition. Slowly, we begin to try it. It's a little like taking a new car out on the highway. The same tension that we experience steering an unfamiliar vehicle down the expressway affects us during the assimilation of change. There is always the underlying fear that we'll crash or fail and have to suffer the consequences. Slowly, our confidence builds as we learn how to drive the unfamiliar vehicle or use the change condition to our advantage.

Ask yourself these questions if you are beginning to ASSIMILATE your change condition:

- Although you still dislike the change, are you beginning to use aspects of it in your daily work?

- Do you consciously try to use the new patterns or procedures?

- Do you occasionally have an "ah hah!" moment when your use of the change has been successful?

## Step Four: Transference

Eventually, as we continue to assimilate the change condition, we enter into the TRANSFERENCE stage. The new technology, thoughts, processes and procedures replace the old. We still feel a sense of uneasiness and discomfort as we learn to make this replacement or transference. Part of us still longs to return to the old way because we felt comfortable and in control, but we know that there is no turning back.

As we transfer the change, we begin to appreciate its positive impact. We no longer view it as an enemy, but rather as a new friend to get to know better and to use whenever possible.

Are you at the TRANSFERENCE step? Ask yourself these questions:

- Do you consciously look for ways to use the change condition to replace former methods or procedures?

- Do you feel a growing sense of satisfaction and confidence as the change works for you?

- Are you becoming an advocate of the change, rather than a resister?

## Step Five: Integration

In the INTEGRATION stage, we finally have accepted the change and work with it comfortably. In fact, we hardly can remember what it was like before the change. Sometimes we wonder how we ever put up with "the old way." We feel confident and once again in control as we use the change daily.

The final step of INTEGRATION is recognized easily by asking ourselves these questions:

- Do you feel comfortable with the change condition?

- Do you feel confident as you use the change in your daily work?

- Do you find it hard to remember what it was like before the change?

Going through these five steps to deal with change is inevitable. We may spend weeks at one stage and minutes at another, but we need to work our way through them whenever we fear and feel threatened by change conditions. They are not comfortable steps. They are not enjoyable ones. But they serve as a proven pathway to coping with the challenge of change.

## What Keeps Us Going?

What keeps us going through it all? Obviously, the fact that change does not go away is a key factor. The change remains, and we are the ones who must deal with it. Throughout the discomfort of stress, uneasiness, uncertainty and doubt, we hang in there. There are four main reasons why we do it: challenge, personal satisfaction, rewards and fear.

### Challenge

Some people see change as a challenge. They enjoy facing new situations and working outside of their comfort zones. For them, change is interesting, exciting and an opportunity to stretch their wings and fly over unexplored territory. When the new computers arrive on their desks, they are challenged by the opportunity to work with something they haven't tried before. They look forward to the learning adventure.

### Personal Satisfaction

Others welcome change as a growth experience. They use the change condition to empower themselves. As they successfully deal with the change, their self-confidence and self-esteem are reinforced. They enjoy the opportunity to use their self-control and self-reliance. They will tell you how much better they are personally after dealing with a condition of change. As they learn to use the new computers in new and different areas of their work, they feel a great deal of personal satisfaction from the learning experience.

## Rewards

There are others who look to the rewards that change may bring. They see the opportunities that may unfold suddenly, and they are quick to take advantage of them. As they work through the change condition, they keep their "eyes on the prize" — whatever reward they expect from successful integration of the change. They know that their newly acquired computer skills will give them more speed, more flexibility and more time.

## Fear

Some only keep going for fear of being left behind, of losing out or missing the boat. They feel no real commitment to the change condition. If possible, they rather would have the change fail, and if the change encounters difficulties, they are the first to express the "I told you so" attitude. They agree to try the computer technology only because everyone else is using it. They are convinced that computers won't be able to deal with their particular tasks, and they feel vindicated if the work falls behind.

## Finding the Fear Factor

If you are aware that you fit into this last category of fear, there is a way that you can determine where your fear of change comes from. From that point, you can deal with the root of your fear and move toward delivering challenge, satisfaction and rewards from change.

Consider your present change condition and think through the following questions.

- What advantages does change offer you?

- What possible rewards might there be if you managed the change successfully?

Be daring. Look at the outcome through rose-colored glasses. Often, it is our own worst-case scenario that creates fear. Looking at the best-case scenario can provide to you the impetus to deal with change as a challenge.

A realistic examination of your comfort zone also can be helpful.

- How is your comfort zone being stretched by the change?

- What areas of your life will this change actually affect?

- What do you do now that you won't be able to do after this change?

- What comfortable habits or practices are being challenged by this change?

- What will you have to give up?

By looking at your comfort zone realistically, you often will find that your fear is based on your desire to remain in a comfortable rut. If you are willing to work with the change, gradually allowing it to move you beyond your usual boundaries, you will begin to experience the personal satisfaction that change can bring.

Use past experiences to help you evaluate how you will deal with this new change.

- Have you ever experienced anything like this change before?

- Is there any other part of your life that could be seen as a parallel to this change condition, no matter how small?

- What experiences from the past are you using to deal with this situation?

- Is there a pattern to the way that you handle change?

Sometimes we allow our past experiences to color our present reality. It's kind of like driving a car by looking through the rear view mirror! If you have had a bad experience with change in the past, you might be bringing those negative emotions and reactions to your present change condition.

Try to look at the change condition as a positive in your life.

- Look at the possible rewards that you could accrue.

- Look at your expanding limits.

- Look at the opportunities to expand your knowledge.

- Look at the possibilities for increasing your self-confidence and self-esteem.

Put the fear behind you and make a conscious determination that **this time you will steer the change vehicle where you want it to go!**

# 5

## HOW TO SURVIVE A CHANGING ORGANIZATION

"It's just not like it used to be in this organization. Everything has changed!" These may be familiar words. The fact is, we must cope with changes in our job descriptions, changes in our departmental responsibilities, changes in our budgets, changes in our reporting lines, changes in our authority, changes in our staffs, changes in our resources, changes in our salaries, changes in our security, changes in our priorities and changes in our expectations.

What has happened to the organization that we knew and were accustomed to?

## Changing Organizational Attitudes

One of the changes that seems to incite the most fear in people is the change in the underlying attitudes of an organization. In our current uncertain economy, many organizations are beginning to look at economies of scale as a way to deal with a tough marketplace. They are downsizing, merging, restructuring and retrenching. The free-wheeling mood of the '70s has given way to the sober second-thoughts of the '90s. Organizations continually are looking for ways to improve their cash flows, conserve their resources and remain competitive.

"Do more with less" has become the battle cry of the '90s. Organizations claim that they want to be "lean and mean." They talk about trimming the fat, cutting out the frills and reallocating resources. It all boils down to a change condition that can be perceived either as an opportunity or a threat.

## Changing Organizational Structures

There was a time when an organizational chart showed a neat array of boxes, each indicating an officer and his organizational departments. Once drawn, this chart became a fixed part of the organization's rule book, remaining in use for years at a time.

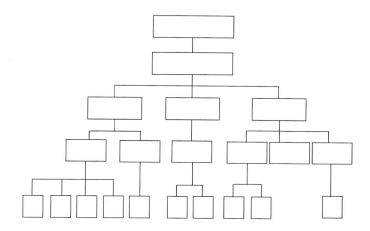

Today, organizational lines are redrawn so frequently that any chart older than three months often is considered antiquated!

Organizations now change their internal structures with dizzying frequency. Titles change from week to week; jobs are transformed; reporting lines are erased and redrawn; responsibilities shift; departments and divisions disappear only to reappear in new guises.

## Changing Individual Roles

Part of this reshuffling can be blamed on the mergers and acquisitions that have become common in today's marketplace. But it is also the result of the changing understanding of an individual's role in the organization. An employee's relationship with any one department or division within the organization is often short-lived. With each restructuring, a new relationship is formed. Today the average individual is reassigned or shuffled from one department to another with alarming frequency. Even if the department remains the same, often the job functions undergo radical changes.

## Changing Hierarchical Lines

The original organizational charts invariably showed the corporate hierarchy as an elongated pyramid. The executives occupied the narrow top range, while the middle managers were in the buffer area between those at the top and the broad bottom layer of line workers. At one time, the average ratio of supervisors to workers in America was one to 10. Today, the pyramid is flattening as organizations restructure to emulate the Japanese model of one supervisor to 100 workers. Increasingly, the middle group is being squeezed out!

## Changing Middle Management Expectations

The middle group is taking the brunt of restructuring. It is expected to do more with less:  fewer people, fewer resources and less authority. Middle managers work in the areas where redundancies most often are declared and where retraining may be the only route to job security.

Part of this retraining may involve technology. To do more with less, many organizations are using electronic tools to streamline workflow, increase productivity and eliminate duplication of effort. To survive, this middle group of the pyramid must deal with the change condition of TECHNOLOGY. This change demands that they learn how to use modern electronic tools: everything from word processors to fax machines to computerized robots for manufacturing.

## Changing Work Assignments

Once an organization has decided to begin restructuring to become more efficient or more competitive, work assignments will change as well. People will find themselves faced with more responsibility, but ironically, they will have less authority than before.

One of the chief causes of workplace stress is responsibility without authority. In a study of so-called high-stress jobs, the researchers surprisingly found that emergency room doctors in large city hospitals and air-traffic controllers at busy airports actually experienced less stress than office workers. Why? Because these doctors and air-traffic controllers could deal authoritatively with the situations that faced them. They could make decisions that were implemented instantly. Office workers, on the other hand, often need to get permission, go through channels or follow the proper line of authority before they can deal with their stressful situations.

## How to Survive Restructuring and Reduce Stress: Six Essential Linking Strategies

As those in the middle begin to feel the effects of restructuring within the organization, they also begin to experience increasing stress. How can these people use the change of restructuring effectively and decrease their stress?

### Linking Strategies

Evaluating the six essential linking strategies will help them deal with the process. One strategy links to the next, until each person reaches the place where he can begin to deal with the change on an individual basis. The six strategies are:

1. Market/customer understanding

2. Strategic thinking/work innovation

3. Diagnostic skills

4. Business/financial understanding

5. Interpersonal group skills

6. Self-management

## Linking Strategy One: Market/Customer Understanding

Any change that affects an organization also must be looked at in terms of how it will affect customers. When restructuring takes place, people often are so busy thinking about themselves that they forget about customers.

The person who sees change as a limit-widening condition immediately will look for opportunities to make the change serve the customer even better than before. Unfortunately, many of us automatically assume that the customer will suffer from our restructuring. Because we are uncomfortable with the process, we deliberately close our eyes to the situation. If our rejection of the change causes a customer to be lost, it is a confirmation of our negative feelings. "I knew that would happen" becomes a self-fulfilling prophecy.

### Example

In the past, you may have visited your customer personally on a monthly basis. Now, because of a restructuring that has given you more responsibilities and less time for those personal visits, your customer service activity will have to change. Of course, you can sit back and announce that the customer isn't going to like the change and may take his or her business elsewhere. Or, you can look for other ways to provide the same or a similar level of service to the customer.

Try to look dispassionately at the restructuring. Remove your negative emotions from the equation and ask yourself some questions.

- How is my customer (either internal or external) going to suffer?

- How can I bridge the gap between the customer's expectations based on past experience and the realities of our present level of service?

- What can I do to ensure that the customer is not the victim of our restructuring?

- How can I take a lead in demonstrating to others in the organization that we can continue to keep our customers satisfied?

The answers to these questions will form a strategy to position you as leader during the restructuring. More importantly, for those who make promotional decisions, you become an outstanding example of someone who "sees the big picture" and who can "roll with the punches." These may not be the exact phrases that appear on your performance appraisal, but the recognition of your strategic thinking will.

## Linking Strategy Two: Strategic Thinking/Work Innovation

As you begin to assess how you can serve your customers best during restructuring, you will begin to see how to be innovative about your particular work functions and assignments.

### Example

Let's go back to the customer who is used to seeing you every month. If your organization is doing more with less, it probably means that you don't have the personnel to assign someone else to visit the customer on a monthly basis. But, if you compare costs, you may find that you can arrange a monthly or even weekly telephone call to that customer. The call actually costs less and still allows you the same contact time. In fact, you may be able to arrange conference calls with other department heads who also deal on a regular basis with the customer. Now the customer is being served by even more people than before.

Innovations like this will involve some strategic thinking and work on your part.

- You must decide what customer needs can be met by a telephone call and if any require a face-to-face encounter.

- You must determine how to present this change to your customers so that they see it as a continuation of attentive service.

- You must map out a schedule that allows you to make the weekly phone calls and still handle your increased responsibilities.

- You must involve the other department heads and personnel.

- You must convince others to spend time with your customers.

- Finally, you must devise a yardstick to measure the effectiveness of the new customer service.

These steps involve strategic thinking and work innovation. It means, quite simply, that you start with an idea and carry it through to its logical conclusion, inventing strategies to make it work and tools to measure its success.

## Linking Strategy Three: Diagnostic Skills

The tools that you use to measure the effectiveness of your work innovations invariably will lead you to use your diagnostic skills. "What gets measured gets done," goes the old saying. Or, as IBM tells its people, "Measurement is the heart of any improvement process. If something cannot be measured, it cannot be improved."

There are three basic tenets to any kind of measurement process:

1. **Measurement must begin at the onset of the program.** Too often, we wait until we've gotten used to certain ways of doing things before we find out if they are really effective.

2. **Measurement should be visible.** Put it on paper and keep permanent records. Don't just rely on a "gut feeling."

3. **Measurement should be stated in the customer's terms.** What does the customer expect? What does the customer need? What works best for the customer? This is a radical departure from our normal way of measuring everything from the point of view of the organization. For example, many sales organizations want their salespeople to keep track or measure how many times they visit a customer. This enables an organization to compare the cost of the salesperson's time with actual sales. However, few organizations measure the effectiveness of the call in terms other than sales. A sales call can be measured from the customer's viewpoint. Did the customer learn anything new about the company or product? Did the customer have an opportunity to try out a product? Did the customer receive a new catalog? Opportunities like these can lead to future sales on subsequent visits.

Once you have measured your customers'
response/satisfaction against your strategic thinking
and work innovation, use the data to diagnose and
then deal with any areas where the data show that
something else should be done.

Measurement will point out any trouble spots. Your
diagnostic strategies will evaluate those areas, pinpoint
the problems, create the solutions and implement a
plan of action.

## Linking Strategy Four: Business/Financial Understanding

When he was mayor of Baltimore, Don Schaefer had a
sheet of paper taped to the wall of his office. On it
was the following list:

#1. PEOPLE

#2. Do It Now

#3. Do It Right The First Time

#4. Do It Within Budget

#5. Would You Like to Live There?

This is a truly customer-oriented list. You must clear all
five of these hurdles to be successful when dealing
with a restructuring in your organization.

Let's examine the fourth point:  doing it within budget. The business equation is simple: Profit equals revenue minus expenses. When expenses exceed revenue, there is no more profit — and usually no more organization. We don't work to keep costs down for the health of the organization;  we do it for our own corporate well-being. Without the organization, we no longer would have jobs!

Your diagnostic strategies are only as good as their financial viability. The challenge is to create strategies that still can meet the budget. There is always a way to overcome the "We can't afford to do that" attitude of many change resisters. Don't allow yourself to adopt the tunnel-vision thinking of those who can't see beyond the usual ways of doing things.

**Example**

Create some innovative, yet cost-effective strategies using the customer visit example.

- Can't visit the customer every month because of restrictions on travel time?

    Call once a week.

- Can't call once a week because of budget cutbacks on long-distance charges?

    Send a friendly note.

- Haven't got time to handwrite 60 notes?

  Create a monthly newsletter that keeps you in touch with customers.

- Can't afford paper, postage and the labor needed to produce a newsletter?

  Arrange for sample copies of related magazines or organizational newsletters to be sent on your behalf.

Keep thinking beyond where you are now, until you reach a point where you are comfortable with the level of service and with the budget.

## Linking Strategy Five: Interpersonal Group Skills

At this point, you must involve others in your strategies. Here's where you need to support the organization's restructuring actively. It's a lot easier to join the ranks of the "Isn't it awfullers" who sit back and wait for all their dire predictions to come true. It's a lot harder to work through the linking strategies that will enable the changes in the organization to provide even better customer service than before. One reason it is more difficult is that you are going up against people who are truly fearful and resist change. They don't want the changes to work. They will do all they can to ensure that they don't work.

If you can show these people how to make the changes work and if you can give them some vision of what can be done, you will find them less fearful.

Let them know your specific goals. What are you planning to do for customers? You may find that they have some information that can speed the effort, and that they may have some ideas you haven't considered. Improved communication and shared information make for strong team-building, better morale, common goals and superb customer service.

## Linking Strategy Six: Self-Management

All of these linking strategies bring us to the final and vital link: self-management. To work through the linking strategies, it is necessary for you to be committed to the organization's restructuring. This commitment goes far beyond passive acceptance. It means that you must be willing to think through the strategies and, more importantly, take the time and effort to put them in place. You'll need a great deal of self-management to accomplish this, because implementing strategies takes time, effort and determination. Sometimes, it will seem easier just to let the change manage itself!

You also need to realize that in any restructuring, your first link of market/customer understanding will elicit many different strategies that may completely change your work role. This can be a radical change for people who always have worked within the tight framework of a job description.

## Example

> Consider an internal customer, such as your shipping/receiving department. If you work through a strategy that allows it to offer the same service level after the restructuring, you may need to initiate procedures that actually require some shipping and receiving functions on your part. If you are tied to your job description, you may not be able to convince yourself that a shipping and receiving function should be part of your job.

But if you truly are committed to coping with the challenge of restructuring, you will see how changing your job function offers you the opportunity to grow and to learn new skills.

**From management's standpoint, you become one of those rare people who is able to handle multiple priorities, effectively deal with issues, and is flexible, proactive and efficient. These are perfect phrases to describe the characteristics of a successful change manager!**

# 6

## REALITIES OF ORGANIZATIONAL CHANGE YOU CAN'T ESCAPE

You may have reached a point where you believe that nothing is predictable in today's changing organization. Yesterday's carved-in-stone edicts that you followed so faithfully are thrown out the window by today's latest change. It's harder to keep up with what is expected of you because everything from your usual working style to your reporting relationships has changed.

Take heart. You can predict some things in organizational change. There are nine predictable conditions that result from the organizational changes around you. By understanding these conditions and adapting to them, you have an edge on change management. You can predict:

- More accountability

- Greater need for leadership

- Greater emphasis on teamwork

- Intense involvement with people

- Greater ambiguity concerning authority

- Greater emphasis on individuality

- Increased involvement of the whole person

- More stress

- Continual learning

In today's organization, the ongoing conditions of change mean that these nine realities exist as part of the change. These realities are often paradoxes in terms of what is expected of the employees and what employees need to survive a change.

## Reality One: More Accountability

The faceless, nameless bureaucrat is gone! Today people are held accountable for their actions and their job performances. Goals are set, and they are expected to be met. Performance standards are not flexible. Each person in today's organization must:

- Meet pre-set goals

- Meet performance standards

- Be proactive in meeting the goals and standards

Each person in today's organization is:

- Accountable to the team

- Accountable to management

- Accountable to self

## Reality Two: Greater Need for Leadership

Management no longer can hide behind closed office doors. Never before has the concept of Management By Walking Around (MBWA) been more relevant. The leaders of today's changing organization must be able to:

- Challenge people with a clearly defined vision

- Motivate people with internal rewards (words and recognition that build self-esteem)

- Communicate with information and feedback

- Listen carefully and constantly

## Reality Three: Greater Emphasis on Teamwork

Not only have the anonymous employee and the hidden manager disappeared, so has the "lone wolf." The person who wants to be an eagle, soaring far above the rest, will find today's changing organization a difficult place in which to fly alone. The emphasis is on teamwork. Members of the team are:

- Accountable to one another

- Self-managing

- Task-oriented

To be an effective team, members should:

- Meet at least once a week

- Work in team groups of no more than 15 people

- Develop their own goals and performance indicators

## Reality Four: Intense Involvement with People

It is not organizations, but people who deal with employees, customers, suppliers, the community and the media. People dealing with people is the basis of

any successful business. To achieve success, people
within an organization should expect to:

- Receive affirmation of their strengths and skills

- Receive encouragement for their struggles

- Receive rewards for positive contributions

This support works both ways. In return, people
within the organization should be involved intensely
with other each by:

- Providing clear leadership where needed

- Offering information and advice on subjects in
  which they have knowledge or expertise

- Contributing their own vision and ideas to the
  organization

- Encouraging and training those who need
  assistance

## Reality Five: Greater Ambiguity Concerning Authority

The corporate hierarchy was created so that
employees would know their places and the limits of
their authority. At the top of the pyramid lay the most
authority, usually vested in the hands of people who
were often traditional, invisible, impersonal and
generally out of touch with the people at the bottom
of the pyramid. Communication took place from the

top down, usually in the form of bureaucratic rules, procedures, regulations and standards. Very little, if any, communication was expected from the bottom up.

The new organizational pyramid doesn't work that way. In some organizations, it's even called an *inverted pyramid* because:

- People from the top are walking around, getting in touch and talking to people at all levels

- People at the bottom feel safe in talking to those at other levels in the pyramid and passing on information and ideas

- Middle managers act as communication conduits, both vertically and horizontally

As a result, the old hierarchical lines of authority are blurred now. More people outside of the top slice of the pyramid are empowered to act with authority whenever necessary. They can:

- Make an immediate decision to take care of a dissatisfied customer without getting permission first

- Have spending authority over amounts that are no longer insultingly low, but reflect the scope of their responsibilities

- Change, circumvent, reinvent and avoid the rules and regulations if it means getting the job done

In other words, they are empowered with the authority to meet their goals.

## Reality Six: Greater Emphasis on Individuality

Because no two people are the same, today's changing organization is beginning to see each employee as an individual with specific needs. This can be seen in:

- Work-sharing programs

- Flexible scheduling

- Individual and team goals

- Training and retraining programs

- Opportunities for lateral movement

## Reality Seven: Increased Involvement of the Whole Person

Because employees are seen as individuals, not just as numbers, they are expected to bring a personal commitment to the organization. This personal commitment can take the form of:

- Voluntary overtime to finish a task

- Participation on special task forces or teams

- Voluntary education in areas relating to the job

## Reality Eight: More Stress

Not unexpectedly, change in an organization causes
more stress among its members. Someone once coined
the phrase, FUD Factor, to describe the reasons for
this increased stress.

### F = FRUSTRATION

There is always some degree of frustration as
people try to work through the new changes that
affect their daily lives. If procedures, job
guidelines, expectations or the direction of the
organization are changed, the employees must
work through the change by experimentation. Like
all experiments, some are successful and some fail.
These initial failures, as people try, try and try
again, lead to frustration.

### U = UNCERTAINTY

No matter how much is communicated about a
change — the reasons, the whys, the wherefores
and even the hows — a certain degree of
uncertainty still exists. Until change happens,
employees don't know if it really will succeed and
whether they really will survive.

### D = DOUBT

And at the back of employees' minds, there are
those little nagging doubts. Maybe this isn't the
right direction, maybe this isn't the right change, or
maybe the old way was better after all.

Only successful integration of the change into the organization's daily life will eliminate the FUD Factor.

## Reality Nine: Continual Learning

The information explosion in today's world means that we never can sit back and announce that we've learned all we'll ever need to know. In fact, that same information explosion compels us to embrace the concept of lifelong learning. Everyday, the change condition challenges us because:

- There is always something new to be learned

- What you learned yesterday may be out of date already

- Only continual learning will keep you in the game

- Lifelong learning must become a daily habit

As you work through the changes in your organization, these predictable realities are the touchstones for your own successful change management. Empowering yourself to move into areas outside the comfort zone of your former work expectations will create a heightened sense of personal responsibility.

While the changing organization generates these realities, only you can make the decision to be accountable, to take a leadership role and to become a team player. Unfortunately, you also must deal with the stresses that this personal role may produce.

# 7

## HOW DO YOU
## HANDLE CHANGE?

We've seen how change can affect an organization and
its employees, but how do you personally handle
change? We all have our own change profile. This
chapter will help you identify yours. For instance, bell
curves long have been used to illustrate changes in a
specific characteristic. Two of the following charts
have an amazing similarity.

The first chart shows the productivity level of three
kinds of employees. The second chart reflects the
performance levels of people exposed to stress. In
each chart, there is a middle ground where people
function in an optimum state: Productivity is high and
stress is low, so peak performance is the norm. During
change, stress affects productivity in people who are
having difficulty dealing with change and who are
threatened by it.

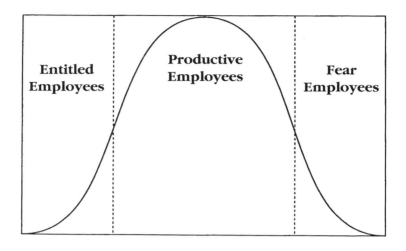

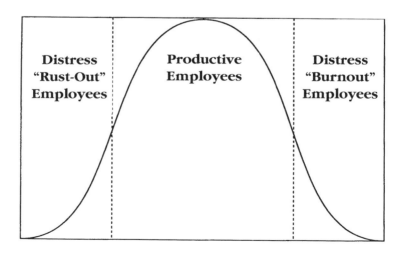

## The Entitlement-Driven Person

At one end of the productivity curve are the entitled persons. These employees truly feel that an entitlement goes along with a job:

- Good pay

- Reasonable job security

- Stability and routine

Their main goal in life is to maintain the status quo. For them, any deviation from "the way we've always done it" is suspect and, therefore, grounds for distrust. They will be the first to resist any sort of change within an organization.

These employees always have managed to survive by risk-avoidance tactics. They like to "play it by the book." In fact, they are always familiar with the rules and regulations of the organization and can quote chapter and verse of any written procedure. Their power resides in bureaucracy, and they expect everyone else to conform to the inherent standards, rules, guidelines, procedures, regulations and red tape. For them, conformity is a protective shell.

Entitled employees avoid any kind of assessment.

- They don't want to set goals, much less meet those goals.

- They don't want to measure their work against anyone else's.

- They don't want to meet the standards deemed necessary by a supervisor.

- They'll engage in any kind of performance appraisal with apathy by saying nothing and doing nothing!

When you look at these people on the stress diagram, you can see that they are working in a state of "rust out." No new ideas, no innovations, no risk taking.

**Do you react to change as an entitled person?**

To determine if you are an entitlement-driven person, ask yourself these four questions:

1. Do you believe that a guideline or procedure should be written before the change occurs?

2. Do you resent performance appraisals that go beyond your specific duties and talk about things like proactive skills, risk taking and initiative?

3. Do you fear that change will make it difficult for you to carry on in your present position and in the way you've always done things in the past?

4. Do you suspect that change is management's way of shaking things up?

## The Fear-Driven Person

The No. 1 priority for fearful employees is self-protection. They always see change as an:

- Economic threat — loss of job

- Psychological threat — loss of security

- Social threat — loss of power or authority

Because they see change as a threat, these people always react with fear. That fear causes them to be dependent upon leadership when they encounter change. They want someone else to tell them what to do, how to do it, when to do it and why.

Unfortunately for the fear-driven employee, this translates to lack of initiative on a performance appraisal and begins a vicious cycle. Those who are fear-driven are made even more fearful when their change behavior does not elicit approval from management. They retreat into apathy and passivity. Instead of becoming proactive, they fall back on their old habits and waste valuable time and effort "covering themselves." A steady stream of paperwork follows: letters, memos, reports, anything that will provide protection should the fear-driven person be held accountable.

The stress diagram shows that the fear-driven person is probably approaching burnout. Although we often associate burnout with overwork, in this case, it comes from overanxiety. The fear-driven person is anxious about everything — from a frown on a supervisor's face to a notice on the bulletin board!

## Are you a fear-driven person?

To determine if you are fear-driven, ask yourself these questions:

1. Do you worry excessively about making a mistake when trying to deal with change?

2. Do you make sure that you cover yourself completely for every action that you take?

3. Do you see change as a threat: economic, psychological or social?

## The Productive Person

Productive people work from a base of security. They feel secure, not necessarily in their jobs, but in their own abilities and skills. They know they can handle whatever is thrown at them. When they are faced with change, they do not see it as either a threat or a promise. They simply take the change at face value and use it to increase their productivity.

Their morale is usually high because they trust the leadership that has instituted the change. They are aware of being part of the team, and they know that their contribution to the change will make a difference in its success or failure.

Often change works as a catalyst, producing peak performances from these people. They work best when they are challenged and motivated to deal with conditions that stretch their abilities and move them outside of their comfort zones.

On the stress chart, these productive people work at peak performance. Change provides the stimulation to keep them there.

**Are you someone who is stimulated by change?**

To determine if you are a productive person, ask yourself these three questions:

1. Do you welcome the challenge that comes with any sort of change? Do you feel empowered by that challenge?

2. Do you respect the leader behind the change? Do you trust their motives?

3. Do you feel a comradeship with your co-workers? Do you see yourself as a vital part of a larger whole?

If you want to deal with change successfully, you need to recognize your individual change profile. If that profile indicates you are either entitlement- or fear-driven, you may want to examine the reasons why you think about change in those contexts. You also may want to remind yourself that being either entitlement- or fear-driven means that you are putting yourself under extra stress and hampering your productivity. It is only when you allow yourself to be stimulated by change that you work at peak performance.

# 8

---

# TAKING THE RISK OUT OF YOUR CHANGE PROJECT

You may feel that change is imposed upon you by others, but there are changes that you impose upon yourself. When you see how a change will benefit the organization or when you have been instructed to fix a problem, you become the instigator of change. You play the role of change agent — the one who must implement the change.

## Risk Factors for Your Project

Regardless of the course of action you choose to implement the change, certain factors will determine its success or failure. By assessing these factors before committing yourself to a particular course of action, you will be prepared for any risks that the change may bring.

## Risk Factor One: Support of Upper Management

The evidence shows conclusively that change always occurs from the top down, never from the bottom up. To be successful, all change should not only have an agent, but also a sponsor — someone with the knowledge, commitment and authority to see that the change is implemented. The most important attribute of the sponsor is authority. That person (or persons) must be able to support the change with organizational authority. Without this support, the change faces great risk of failure.

Before you begin your change project, ask yourself these three questions:

1.  Is there at least one person in upper management who supports this change?

2.  Is this person willing to use authority to make sure that the change is accepted?

3.  Will this person delegate authority to the change agent to ensure the success of the project?

If the answer to any one of these questions is "No," then you should try to persuade someone in upper management to assume a position of authority on the project before you go any further.

## Risk Factor Two: Popularity

If a project is popular with a majority of employees, it has a much higher possibility of success. When a project is disliked, unwanted or even distrusted, the project will meet with resistance, both passive and aggressive. Trying to push through an unpopular project takes a great deal more time and energy, and it often results in greater stress levels for everyone concerned. If the popularity of the project could be a risk factor, ask yourself these questions:

1.  Do the majority of people want this project?

2.  Do the majority of people agree that this project is needed?

3.  Do the majority of people actively support this project?

If you have any negative answers, it might be wise to bring more people on your side before beginning to implement the project.

## Risk Factor Three: Clear Objectives

One of the reasons why people do not support a project is that the objectives are unclear. People distrust what they do not understand. If the objectives are not defined clearly, people will give their own interpretations to the project. To be sure that the objectives are clear, ask yourself these three questions:

1. Can I write the project objectives in one sentence?

2. Do the objectives mean the same things to all people?

3. Have the objectives been discussed or explained so that everyone understands them?

Sometimes, you can clarify objectives by trying to state them in one sentence. This forces you to avoid jargon, business-ese, platitudes and fuzzy thinking. It brings you to the bottom line of why you're implementing the change.

## Risk Factor Four: Agreement

You may have been able to state your objectives in one sentence, but if there is no agreement on these objectives among the users and management, then the project is unlikely to get off the ground. For example, you may want to introduce a new way of training customers to use your company's product. Your objective is to reduce the number of call backs that you need to make to assist customers. However, if management sees these call backs as a way to supply service visibly to the customer, you have a disagreement on objectives. Your training project is in trouble before it begins. To determine if you have agreement on objectives, ask yourself these three questions:

1.  Who — management, users or both — will benefit most from these objectives?

2.  Who — management, users or both — will perceive these objectives as nonbeneficial?

3.  Who — management, users or both — is likely to resist these objectives?

If you answer either management or users in any of the three questions, then you probably will disagree on the project's objectives. The solution is not to change the project, but to change the objectives. In the previous example, change the objective to increased customer service through more effective training programs. Both user and management will agree on this objective.

## Risk Factor Five: Budget

Everything still comes back to the bottom line: "Can we afford it?" Nothing will derail a change more quickly than lack of funds to implement it effectively. Taking funds from some other area to finance the change will create a great deal of distrust and unpopularity for the change. Be honest and assess your project's budget using the following three questions:

1.  Taking all possible contingencies into account, how much is this change really going to cost?

2. Do we have that much money?

3. If not, how are we going to get it?

Never try to implement change on a shoestring budget! It's a little like building a new house without the money for plumbing or electricity. You end up with a shell that is unlivable. Even worse, you end up with visible evidence of your failure.

## Risk Factor Six: Time

It seems there's never time to do it right the first time, but there's always time to do it over again. CHANGE TAKES TIME. This is one of the hardest lessons you can learn. No matter how well-prepared you are, how much you have invested in the change or how many contingency plans you've made, it always takes longer than you expected. One of the reasons that change takes time is that change involves people, and people need time to integrate change. People also are unpredictable. Those whom you have selected to be your change advocates may be the ones who have the most difficulty assimilating the change. Those from whom you expected support may resist the change passively. Time is your only ally when dealing with change. Over time, all change becomes reality.

Consider how long it took to change our attitudes about smoking. In 1957, the Surgeon General announced that cigarettes were dangerous to our health. Back then it was believed that this announcement instantly would trigger a change in smoking habits. Actually, it has taken nearly 35 years for society to begin to change its attitude toward cigarette smoking!

## Risk Factor Seven: People

When you are the change agent for a particular project, you must consider the people who will implement your change. Certainly, it would be much easier if we could do it ourselves, but in today's team-oriented organization, everyone has a responsibility to act as a change agent. Therefore, think about the people who will be involved. Ask yourself these questions:

1.  **Are they enthusiastic?** We can't expect everyone to stand up, wave pompoms and lead a cheer for change, but enthusiasm does play a large role in the success of change. A lukewarm attitude often is more dangerous than downright resistance. Lukewarm people subtly sabotage change simply through passive lack of enthusiasm. They won't say, "I hate what is happening." Instead, they'll say, "Oh, it's all right, I guess, sort of, if you like that kind of thing...," and then do nothing. They won't tell you if there are problems because they don't even notice them. They won't give you any suggestions because they don't have any. They won't advocate the change publicly because they don't really care.

2. **Do they have adequate time?** People often refuse to change simply because they don't have time. It is a perfectly legitimate reason because the learning curve associated with change always takes time away from their regular schedules. For example, if your project involves computerization of a particular office function, you need to realize that the people currently performing that function must continue to maintain their output even through the change process. This may be impossible! You can counteract this by planning for extra personnel to assist, relaxing current deadlines, reassigning some job functions or authorizing overtime. To demand that people implement change while continuing their normal work schedules is a recipe for failure.

3. **Do they have adequate skills?** Most change involves training of some kind. As soon as we talk about training, the time factor again is important. Training involves three levels:

   1. Knowledge of the skill

   2. Acquisition of the skill

   3. Assimilation of the skill

For example, if you introduce multifunction, touch-tone telephones to replace the old one-line, rotary-dialed phones, people will need training. First, they'll read the manual explaining how to use the new phones (knowledge). Then, they'll try some of the functions (skill). Finally, they'll begin to use the phone with confidence (assimilation). This all takes time. At some point during the implementation of the change, frustration will build as people make mistakes, relearn and then assimilate the new information.

## Risk Factor Eight:  You

The same three questions that you asked about the people around you also apply to you.

1.  Are you enthusiastic?

2.  Do you have adequate time?

3.  Do you have adequate skills?

The same answers will determine whether or not your project for change will be successful. There is, however, one other question that will make a difference to the success or failure of your project:

•  DO YOU HAVE SUFFICIENT AUTHORITY?

The answer here is simply "Yes" or "No." If it is "No," then your project is at risk. Neither your enthusiasm, your energy, popularity, nor your desire will carry a change project to completion if you do not have the authority to MAKE IT HAPPEN.

# 9

# HOW TO SUCCEED IN THE 21ST CENTURY WORKPLACE

We each carry our own particular package of skills, experiences, personal qualities, strengths and weaknesses. Certain combinations of these factors make us more adaptable to change and more likely to cope with it successfully. If we know that change is accelerating in our world today, then we must realize that the ability to adapt to change is one of the most vital components of our package.

## The Personal Aspects of Change

Our ability to adapt to change is based on a fairly loose combination of characteristics that are determined by:

— How we see ourselves

— How we view the world

— How we deal with others and

— How we feel about change

You can determine your change behavior by assessing your particular characteristics based on the following eight aspects of personal behavior.

## Aspect One: Whole-Task Thinking

Whole-task thinking is the opposite of tunnel vision. Rather than concentrating solely on your own particular field of expertise when dealing with a change, you need to see the change and your role in it in terms of the larger picture. There are four approaches to dealing with whole-task thinking. Each depends upon your individual needs. How do you deal with whole-task thinking? Do you:

- Need to explore many different avenues and solutions to the change?

- Need a structured approach to the thinking process?

- Need to find consensus among all the parties involved in the change?

- Need to work with as much information as possible before searching for a solution?

## Aspect Two: Adaptability

Some of us are just more adaptable than others. That is a reality of life. Again, how you adapt is determined by your particular needs. If you are highly adaptable, you probably need:

CHALLENGE — You're always looking for something that stretches you beyond your present comfort zone.

**OR**

VARIETY     — You like to experience as many different things as possible in every aspect of your life.

If you find it difficult to adapt quickly to changing conditions, it may be because you need:

CONTROL     — You feel that you will lose control if the change itself begins to change.

**OR**

SECURITY     — You don't like risk taking and always opt for the known and familiar path.

## Aspect Three: Shared Goals

One of the reasons why organizational hierarchy is changing in today's business world is that more emphasis is being placed on teams and team participation. Being a team player is touted as a premium requirement in management positions. In fact, the lone-eagle mentality often is discouraged in organizations. Where do you fit into the team? Are you:

- Often the leader? You find it easy to persuade people to take your point of view, and you enjoy leading a team toward a shared goal.

- Often at odds with the leader? You find it difficult to allow someone else to lead a group when you don't agree with his point of view.

- Often a valued team member? You enjoy being part of the give-and-take relationship of a true team. You appreciate others' ideas and opinions and seek consensus in shared goals.

- Often uncomfortable with the team concept? You prefer to work independently and then bring your completed part of the task to the team.

## Aspect Four: Tradition

How we feel about tradition will affect how we deal with the conditions of change. We each perceive the relationship between tradition and change differently. Some of us:

- See change as a threat to traditions that are important to us. We believe that tradition is an integral part of our world and that it may be lost. For example, our concept of family, based on the traditional model, may be important to us. We may be uncomfortable with the '90s concept of a "family unit" because it may include nontraditional roles.

- See change as more important than the traditions that may be lost. We're comfortable with new concepts and new ideas, and we don't really miss the traditional ways of thinking.

## Aspect Five: Rewards for Skill Mastery

Part of the concept of change is the need to master new skills. Whether we like it or not, those new skills are crucial to successful change management. The new skill may be as simple as learning to use the automated bank teller or as complex as running a sophisticated computer system. We all work toward skill mastery, but we all have different reasons for doing so.

Some of us are rewarded by:

RECOGNITION — We want to be recognized for
our abilities. We need to
know that our skill mastery
has been noticed by those
who make promotional
decisions. We want that
certificate, that raise or that
title to attest to our skill
mastery.

CONTROL — Some of us learn a new skill
only to regain control. We
want to do it ourselves
without having to rely on
someone else either to do the
work for us or show us how.
Once we have mastered the
skill and are completely in
control of the situation, we
feel comfortable with the
change.

ACCEPTANCE — By mastering the skill, we
gain acceptance from our
peers. We really don't want to
be the only ones who are
unable to handle the change.
We want to be part of the
team, so mastering the skill
allows us to be on an equal
footing with other members.

PERFECTION    — If we are going to master a new skill, we are going to master it correctly. We'll take all the time needed to do it right. For us, the sense of perfection is our reward.

## Aspect Six: Training and Retraining

Unlike skill mastery, which is goal-oriented, training and retraining tend to be an ongoing process. Some people naturally enjoy this process; others do not. If you are:

- Easily bored, impatient with details and seek innovation, then you probably do not enjoy training and retraining.

- Detail-oriented, patient and actively seek information, then you probably train and retrain easily as required by change.

## Aspect Seven:  Access to Information

How we access information or how we come up with ideas is determined by our preferences for idea generation, whether the idea is generated by ourselves or by others.  Do you:

- Really like your own ideas best? You listen to the ideas of others but, by and large, they aren't as good as yours.

- Like creative ideas best? You really appreciate an idea that comes from a different direction or takes an unusual approach.

- Like ideas that are backed by facts and data? You aren't comfortable with ideas that do not have substantive information to back them up.

- Like lots of idea alternatives? You want ideas from as many different sources as possible. You prefer to let others decide which idea is best.

## Aspect Eight:  Cooperation

People cooperate with each other for a variety of reasons. What is your underlying reason for cooperation? Do you believe:

- *We* are important? The group and its point of view come first.

- *I* am important? My point of view and my directions need to be implemented.

- *They* are important? Everyone else's point of view and directions need to be considered and implemented.

- *It* is important? The goal of the group must be met.

These eight personal aspects of change vary from individual to individual. You may be strong in some areas and weak in others. Taken as a whole, they form your package of change-management behaviors. Now that you have identified them, you may wish to concentrate on those where you are weak. Be prepared either to compensate for the weaker aspects or alter your behavior patterns when dealing with change.

# 10

## YOUR PERSONAL ACTION PLAN: COPING WITH TOMORROW TODAY

All the gurus of change agree on one thing: Organizations are changing because of the need to remain competitive in today's marketplace. Successful organizations will have certain common characteristics:

- A flattened organizational pyramid

- Plenty of specialists in the ranks

- Work teams to handle multiple tasks

- Innovative, creative and proactive strategies

- Empowered employees

The importance of all of these characteristics has been discussed.

## The Seven-Point Focus of Change Management

Most importantly, the successful organization will recognize that there are seven points for management to focus on during change. Some of the points have an organizational focus, while others have a more personal focus. The points are:

1. Speed

2. Convenience

3. Quality

4. Technology

5. Service

6. Positioning

7. Continuous improvement

## Speed

Change doesn't wait until people are ready to deal with it. The change vehicle keeps on rolling. Either you get on board and take control, or you get left behind. Change must be assimilated speedily and then integrated as quickly as possible so that you are ready for the next change vehicle in your path. You cannot afford a wait-and-see attitude. It may cause you to miss a vital change opportunity. To assimilate change speedily, you must:

- See change as an opportunity

- Immediately assess how the change can fit into your current work practices

- Envision best-case scenarios for the change in your life

## Convenience

If change will make things difficult, you probably will ignore it by being inactive. Most of us avoid difficulty. We want things to be easy. Change needs to be convenient, rather than difficult.

To do this, you can:

- Assimilate the change a little bit at a time.

- Allow yourself the luxury of working through the change in one area, while keeping in mind the need for speedy assimilation overall.

- Make a list of all the things that could be done more easily once the change is integrated. Use this as your motivator when you feel bogged down.

## Quality

At no time should the quality of your product or service be compromised as you work through a change. This is one of the most difficult aspects of change because we know that focusing on speed may damage quality. To ensure that quality control is maintained, you can:

- Define quality from the customer's viewpoint

- Measure quality on an ongoing basis

- Reward contributions to quality improvement

## Technology

Sometimes, when the change vehicle overtakes us, we discover that we do not have the tools we need to handle the change. Simply bringing in technology is not always the answer. New technology means retraining. Retraining results in a learning curve that itself will slow down the change assimilation. You can flatten this curve somewhat by:

- Thinking through the technology carefully and assessing exactly what is needed to handle the changes. Consult the experts. This is a time for specialists.

- Assessing your staff. Who is ready for retraining? Who can be spared to undergo this training? How much time will they need before the technology efficiently addresses the problems brought about by change?

- Being sure that you are committed to a change in technology. You will need to lead by example.

## Service

Most people do not realize that they have two kinds of customers: internal and external. The external customer — the one who buys your product or service — gets the most attention. But the internal customer is equally important. These are the people you deal with daily within your organization:  the shipping department, accounting, sales, customer service and marketing. Although they may not pay for your particular product or service, they do rely on you for timely information and feedback in areas of mutual interest. Make sure that service to your internal customers is not jeopardized by change. Be sure to:

- Maintain communication with these customers. Remember, they are going through change, too, and they may feel equally out of touch.

- Maintain the old methods of communication while you wait to install, learn or develop the new technology required for change. Don't leave a gap in communications.

- Be patient. Change takes time to assimilate. Although you should be aware of the need for speed, don't allow your desire for a quick solution to overlook internal customers.

## Positioning

During change, this can be a purely personal focus for you. Change usually offers those who accept the challenge an opportunity to shine. The opportunity can lead to rewards, recognition and even promotion. It's all in how you position yourself to take advantage of change. You can start positioning yourself today by:

- Beginning a program of retraining. Start where you believe technology, expertise or information will be needed.

- Creating a specialist niche for yourself. Specialize in something. Become an expert. Be the resident guru on that topic.

- Preparing yourself for the change vehicle. Gaze into your personal crystal ball and predict from which direction the change vehicle is likely to come. Get into position, and be ready to steer it where you want to go.

## Continuous Improvement

If we recognize that change is a reality in any living organism and that change demands our attention, we also will realize that change brings about continuous improvement or continuous chaos. Improvement comes from being in control of the change vehicle. Without that control, change will bring continuous chaos. To avoid chaos when faced with change, it's best to:

- Prepare yourself mentally for the change. Begin to think about life after change, rather than dwelling on how life was or how it is now.

- Prepare yourself physically for the change. Be aware that change is a known stress inducer and that your body will react to the stresses. Get plenty of rest, eat well and exercise often.

- Prepare yourself emotionally for the change. Let go of your comfort zone. Release those old confining habits. Begin to experiment by moving beyond the boundaries of your day-to-day experience.

# 11

## WIIFM
## (WHAT'S IN IT FOR ME?)

### A Final Word

Someone once said that the only person who likes change is a wet baby! That may be true. However, if you are involved in the process of change, whether you like it or not, it is essential for you to learn to cope today with the realities of tomorrow.

Ignoring change has two implications for you as a business professional. One is that you may miss out on the opportunities that change offers you — opportunities to grow, to thrive and to succeed in your organization. And two is that you may be left behind as your colleagues take advantage of these same opportunities.

The final question is, "What's in it for me?" The answer is simple: Successful change management is the gateway to future success. If you learn to cope with change successfully, you can soar as high as you can dream!

# Index

# SPECIAL HANDBOOK OFFER

## *Buy two, get one free!*

Each of our handbook series (LIFESTYLE, COMMUNICATION, PRODUCTIVITY, and LEADERSHIP) was designed to give you the most comprehensive collection of hands-on desktop references all related to a specific topic. They're a great value at the regular price of $12.95 ($14.95 in Canada); plus, at the unbeatable offer of buy two at the regular price and get one free, you can't find a better value in learning resources. **To order**, see the back of this page for the entire handbook selection.

1. Fill out and send the entire page by mail to:

**National Press Publications**
6901 West 63rd Street
P.O. Box 2949
Shawnee Mission, Kansas 66201-1349

2. Or **FAX 1-913-432-0824**

3. Or call toll-free **1-800-258-7248** (**1-800-685-4142** in Canada)

Fill out completely:

Name _____

Organization _____

Address _____

City _____

State/Province _____ ZIP/Postal Code _____

Telephone ( ) _____

## *Method of Payment:*

❑ Enclosed is my check or money order

❑ Please charge to:

    ❑ MasterCard   ❑ VISA   ❑ American Express

Signature _____ Exp. Date _____

Credit Card Number

❑ ❑ ❑ ❑ ❑ ❑ ❑ ❑ ❑ ❑ ❑ ❑ ❑

To order multiple copies for co-workers and friends: U.S.   Can.

    20-50 copies...........................................$8.50  $10.95

    More than 50 copies...............................$7.50  $ 9.95

**VIP# 705-008421-093**

# OTHER DESKTOP HANDBOOKS

| | Qty | Item# | Title | U.S. | Can. | Total |
|---|---|---|---|---|---|---|
| **LEADERSHIP** | | 410 | The Supervisor's Handbook, Revised and Expanded | $12.95 | $14.95 | |
| | | 418 | Total Quality Management | $12.95 | $14.95 | |
| | | 421 | Change: Coping with Tomorrow Today | $12.95 | $14.95 | |
| | | 458 | Positive Performance Management *A Guide to Win-Win Reviews* | $12.95 | $14.95 | |
| | | 459 | Techniques of Successful Delegation | $12.95 | $14.95 | |
| | | 463 | Powerful Leadership Skills for Women | $12.95 | $14.95 | |
| | | 494 | Team-Building | $12.95 | $14.95 | |
| | | 495 | How to Manage Conflict | $12.95 | $14.95 | |
| | | 469 | Peak Performance | $12.95 | $14.95 | |
| **COMMUNICATION** | | 413 | Dynamic Communication Skills for Women | $12.95 | $14.95 | |
| | | 414 | The Write Stuff: *A Style Manual for Effective Business Writing* | $12.95 | $14.95 | |
| | | 417 | Listen Up: *Hear What's Really Being Said* | $12.95 | $14.95 | |
| | | 442 | Assertiveness: *Get What You Want Without Being Pushy* | $12.95 | $14.95 | |
| | | 460 | Techniques to Improve Your Writing Skills | $12.95 | $14.95 | |
| | | 461 | Powerful Presentation Skills | $12.95 | $14.95 | |
| | | 482 | Techniques of Effective Telephone Communication | $12.95 | $14.95 | |
| | | 485 | Personal Negotiating Skills | $12.95 | $14.95 | |
| | | 488 | Customer Service: *The Key to Winning Lifetime Customers* | $12.95 | $14.95 | |
| | | 498 | How to Manage Your Boss | $12.95 | $14.95 | |
| **PRODUCTIVITY** | | 411 | Getting Things Done: *An Achiever's Guide to Time Management* | $12.95 | $14.95 | |
| | | 443 | A New Attitude | $12.95 | $14.95 | |
| | | 468 | Understanding the Bottom Line: *Finance for the Non-Financial Manager* | $12.95 | $14.95 | |
| | | 483 | Successful Sales Strategies: *A Woman's Perspective* | $12.95 | $14.95 | |
| | | 489 | Doing Business Over the Phone *Telemarketing for the '90s* | $12.95 | $14.95 | |
| | | 496 | Motivation & Goal-Setting *The Keys to Achieving Success* | $12.95 | $14.95 | |
| **LIFESTYLE** | | 415 | Balancing Career & Family: *Overcoming the Superwoman Syndrome* | $12.95 | $14.95 | |
| | | 416 | Real Men Don't Vacuum | $12.95 | $14.95 | |
| | | 464 | Self-Esteem: *The Power to Be Your Best* | $12.95 | $14.95 | |
| | | 484 | The Stress Management Handbook | $12.95 | $14.95 | |
| | | 486 | Parenting: *Ward & June Don't Live Here Anymore* | $12.95 | $14.95 | |
| | | 487 | How to Get the Job You Want | $12.95 | $14.95 | |

| **SALES TAX** All purchases subject to state and local sales tax. Questions? Call **1-800-258-7248** | |
|---|---|
| **Subtotal** | |
| **Sales Tax** **(Add appropriate state and local tax)** | |
| **Shipping and Handling** **($1 one item, 50¢ each additional item)** | |
| **Total** | |

**VIP#705-008421-093**